Promises
From the Still Small Voice

Promises
From the Still Small Voice

V. Blakeman Vaughn

Darkhorse Press U.S.

Other Books by this Author:
From Here Until Forever, Essays

Large Print Edition
ISBN 978-1-7359781-3-0
PROMtxt060222-30 lrgcx

Darkhorse Press U.S.
New Thought Library
Oakland California
United States

For Charles McGee.
Carpenter, neighbor,
and gentle friend.
I honor your path.

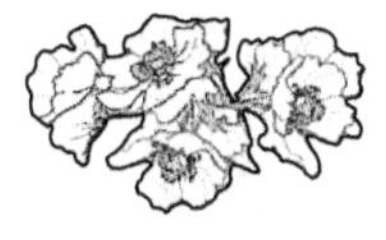

JESUS' PROMISES

"And I will pray the father, and He will give you another counselor to be with you forever, even the Spirit of truth, whom the world cannot receive, because it neither sees him nor knows him. You know him, for he dwells with you, and will be in you."

— John 14: 16-17

"These things I have spoken to you, while I am still with you. But the counselor, the Holy Spirit, whom the Father will send in my name, he will teach you all things, and bring to your remembrance all that I have said to you."

"Peace I leave with you; my peace I give to you; not as the world gives do I give to you. Let not your hearts be troubled, neither let them be afraid."

— John 14: 25-27

"I have yet many things to say to you, but you cannot bear them now. When the Spirit of truth comes he will guide you into all truth, for he will not speak on his own authority, but whatever he hears he will speak. And he will declare to you things that are to come. He will take what is mine and declare it to you."

— John 16: 12–13

PREFACE

You don't have to be anointed or chosen, you are already sacred and you were born chosen. This is the gift already given. I've heard that God speaks to everyone in the way we can personally understand. I believe this, and I believe that the opportunity to receive this is always within us.

The hardest part of this is the surrender, trusting the still small voice because it comes from within, not from a burning bush or other "miracle" and because we often don't see the miracles that are all around us, and commonplace. What is true, sometimes comes quietly. With all the things we must fight and fear and resist in the physical world, trusting seems so risky, and we have been told we should trust ministers, priests, rabbis or other official perceptions, but not our own inner knowing. The Teacher Jesus of Nazareth, said "The kingdom of God is within."

And yet God is also everything that you see, feel, and know. God is all of it, including you. There is no separate identity, but only unique expressions of Life/God/Being, and you, a "self," are one of them. Your life and everything you are, is one manifestation of God into form. You are a way that God expresses and experiences here in this place. God/Life/consciousness is all there is that's real, so separation from all-that-is, can only be a mind-illusion. Our mortal illusions, our beliefs and concepts, are neither wrong nor right, just our own way of playing the game and dancing the dance of Life. There are infinite ways.

You are created not only by God, but of God. The creative and all-knowing unlimited God that is Life Itself has taken innumerable forms for its pleasure and delight, so that God could experience the adventures, challenges, joys and sorrows, limitations and victories of this life, through you, and as you. What you are, in truth, is

God expressing here, God playing, and God dancing.

Rejoice, for you shall dance forever, here now, and someday another way, another place, for there is really no time and place, only life without end. Amen.

It is God's pleasure
to adventure here
as you.

INTRODUCTION

The first time it happened I was shocked and stunned. I didn't know what it was, or where it came from. I was shaken and frightened. I knew something significant was happening, but I had never experienced anything like this, and I had no name for it. I wasn't even sure if it was real. Decades later I would read about similar events in the lives of great people, including lay-people of every kind, scholars. philosophers, scientists, physicists, brilliant minds like the renowned and respected Barbara Marx Hubbard, and ordinary people like myself. But I didn't know it then, and when it happened to me, I had no knowledge of others' experiences of this except things like Bible stories. I could not imagine that this was the same.

This came at a difficult time in my life, and I was seeking guidance wherever I could. Reading a book by John Bradshaw, "Homecoming – Reclaiming the Inner Child," In the book I came across a simple exercise. You are to write a letter to your inner child, tell him or her that you love her, that she is beautiful and good, and that you will always love and protect her, in all the ways her (your) parents may not have been able to do.   The next step of the exercise was to take the pen into your other, left or non-dominant hand, and to answer that letter with a letter FROM that inner child at about age four or five, using the words and the feelings of the little child that you were back then. So I tried it.

Words presented themselves from the inside of me and as they came I wrote them down with my left hand.

They were not from any wisdom of my own, or any book I had read, and not from any voice that could be heard, and yet this was clearly not myself that was creating the sentences. I had always heard that God speaks to each of us in a way that we can personally understand. Maybe because I was a writer, this was the simplest and clearest way for me.

The words came spontaneously, and as my left hand awkwardly formed the letters, my eyes flooded with unexpected tears, which continued without sound and without ceasing while I was writing.

Then when I read what my left hand had written, I was astonished at how intensely personal and painful the words and feelings were. They touched a place in me that had been locked up untouched since I was four years old. In the quiet opening of that place, I saw that I was still the same hurt and abandoned child, unhealed, and I was re-experiencing all of it, not in memory, but in "real-time" and "live."

This was a stunningly profound experience, but I didn't know what to do with it, so I put it away. As time went by, I would write again to my inner child, and again it answered my "letters." Gradually my curiosity turned to trust. I noticed that the kindness and simple wisdom of this voice were far greater than my own. As I began to go more often to this inner source for support and help with things that were going on in my life, the process emerged in a natural way, the voice matured somehow, and in time became a relationship between myself and an entity I came to call the inner Counselor, my own inner counselor as Jesus had promised to His disciples just before He left this earth.

The process is simple, and I believe it can be done by anyone, but with a word of caution: this experience may be profoundly disturbing and is could to be very painful. You should not do it without someone, a source of spiritual or emotional support , available.

Find a place where in a place where you are as safe and warm as possible, and will not be disturbed or interrupted. Spend a little time for meditation or prayer, or whatever feels right for you.

After I've done my prayer meditation, I sit for a while in silence, and then I ask for help and guidance. In something very much like a personal letter on paper, I write out my troubles, fears, and questions to the counselor. Then I take the pen into my other, non-dominant hand, and wait for the answers.

For me, the words come, only two or three at a time, not in full sentences. I don't know what the message is going to say until after it's written. Yet it always comes out making sense; always says things I don't expect, and always tells the truth.

My letters to the Counselor are often confused and searching, pleading, angry at life and circumstances, or feeling lost and frightened. What the Counselor "writes" to me is always wise and calm and loving. Tears often pour down my face as I write, yet there is no sadness and no sound. I feel a vast sense of calm and peace as I sit perfectly still, watching the words spelling themselves out onto the paper in the left-handed scrawl. Each time, I'm amazed by the clarity, simplicity, wisdom and authority that speaks in this way, and the gentleness and kindness of the messages that come. There can be no doubt that they have come from another source, not my ego, not my personality, and not my conscious analyzing mind.

For years I kept this secret, wondering Who is it that speaks? Is it God? Is it Jesus? Sometimes it seemed like it might be His voice, yet who can know what the voice of God is like? And there is no actual sound, just the words forming in my mind for a brief moment as my left-hand writes. I've tried to identify some entity, some source outside of myself. Is it an angel? A spiritual guide? I began to read books by spiritual writers who spoke of such things. I knew that this silent voice that entered into my consciousness when I called was something much more than just my own mind. I believed it could be the inner Counselor that Jesus spoke of, and eventually I accepted this as explanation enough. Even so, I was hesitant to tell anyone, afraid of what they might think. I kept this to myself for more than ten years.

The asking & receiving continued as I blundered through life experiences of all kinds. Physical, emotional, and financial struggles, relationships and losses, successes and failures, a life-threatening illness. Through all of it, I saved the pages of my asking and the Counselor answering in notebooks which nobody ever saw.

And then a tragedy happened. A good friend, my neighbor, was suddenly diagnosed with a terminal illness. He would pass from this earth with the same quiet grace with which he had lived, and in only a few weeks, he was gone. His departure left us all in shock and disbelief. For the first time, I realized that I too might not live as long as I had planned, and if I were destined to do anything meaningful in this life, I had better do it now. I believed these messages I had been given were a gift that now I was being asked to share.

I sorted through about seven years of pages of asking-and-receiving messages from the Counselor. By no more than intuition, I pulled out the ones that called to be chosen, typed them so they would be readable, and then laid them all out on the carpet and allowed them to arrange themselves, again by intuition, chance, or grace, into the order that they now appear in this book, and dedicated the book to Charles, the friend I had lost.

The book does not speak from any authority of my own, and I have left out everything I wrote as I called on God or Universal Mind through the Counselor, as they are not important. I have faithfully included only the answers I received.

The Counselor addressed me either by my own name, or by the name "beloved." In this book, wherever my name appeared in the original words, I have substituted the name beloved throughout.

I believe that these messages were not given only to the person of me alone, but were intended to be shared. I share them now with you in the hope that something here may hold an answer you have needed, as I did. I believe that if this little book has found its way into your hands, then there is a message here that was always intended for you.

V. Blakeman Vaughn,
September 2004

Your treasure is not what you have,
even though you have abundance.
Your value is not what you do,
even though you do
great and wondrous things.
The treasure you have
and the gift you give
is Who You Are.
You are Spirit of Christ,
you are God-in-the-world,
you are Truth in action,
You are Love made manifest.
Remember this.

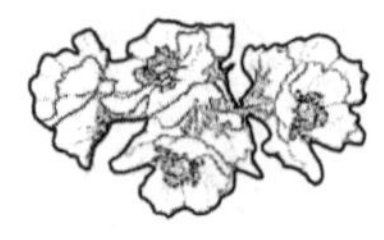

Open every door,
and do not be afraid
of what you will find.
Many doors will open to you.
You have nothing to fear
from any of them,
so long as you are sincere.
Search your heart
and trust what you find there.
Take this adventure and see
where it leads.
Trust God's infinite love for you
and know that whatever you do
honestly
cannot be a mistake.

It is good to help and serve
your brothers and sisters in this world,
because God is in them.
But it is wrong to neglect your own
desires and needs,
because God is in you.
Make no mistake about this:
When you fail to give to yourself,
you are withholding from God
that very thing and only thing
God asks of you:
to live on earth for Him.
Your joy is His joy. Your love is His love.
When you are in sorrow,
the heart of God is in sorrow.
Be not sad or sick or stressed –
be alive with health and love

and Joyfulness.
This is how God wants you
to serve Him – in joy.

This day is yours to live.
I will live it with you, but you must live it.
Express your heart into your world,
and then, whatever happens,
you have expressed Me.
Take each day as it comes,
and hold to the path lightly.
Do not try to understand. You cannot.
Be willing to fail,
if that's what honesty brings.
Come out from behind
the mask you wear
before everyone else but Me.
The eyes of the world
will never know you as I do.
Be willing to fail in the eyes of the world,
and fear not,

for I Am the world,
and all that's in it is but a thought
in the mind of God.

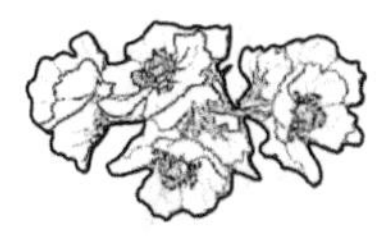

Study your heart;
know what you desire,
and accept the truth that
all you desire,
you fully deserve.
Pray for it believing,
knowing I have it here,
ready for you to ask.
Trust My love to always gift
and bless you
even more and even better than
you have asked.
See your heart clearly.
Refuse compromise.
Do not wait. Do not plan.
Just begin, and trust the universe.

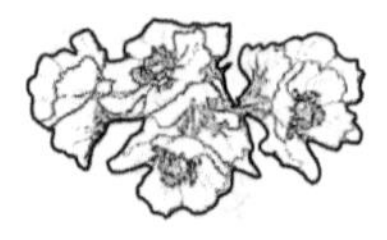

No one earns the love of God
or any other love;
love is always and only a gift.
Do not judge yourself.
I have called your name,
and I have judged you worthy.
There has never been a time
when I did not love you,
and there never will be.
Take courage and take faith,
and you will find the way
to share what you have been given.
Just start giving it.
Just begin to be who you truly are.
That is enough.

Tonight is a place on the journey.
The journey is long, and there are
many adventures open to you.
It is time to make choices and
commitments
and to run through the rain
and dance in the wind.
There is so much more to do,
and so much more to be,
and each thing carries
the great potential
to be joyful.
You could have love, if you would.
You could teach and lead.
All these gifts I have prepared for you,
but you must claim them.

Your work is revealed to you
day by day.
Everything you do and
everything you say,
is part of it.
Any work is an opportunity.
All of life is opportunity.
Choose what gives you joy – now.
Try things on. Discover. Express.
I Am leading You now.
You can walk with confidence.
You can go anywhere, and do anything.
But there is work we have chosen
to do together.
Seek to know it, and when you know it,
put it first above all else,
and I will prosper it.

You have asked,
"How will I know my mission?"
You will know when
you are doing God's work
because you will choose it.
In your heart you have already chosen.
The ways of the world are limited
and limiting.
The way of God is unlimited.
Choose the way of God
and follow it in the world.
Claim the protection God offers you
and you will be safe in the world.
The way will be shown
and the gifts will be given.
You will have help.
You will not do this alone.

You ask who I am.

I am You.

When you write, I write.

When you speak, I speak.

The only impediment to your progress

is within you:

you do not trust yourself.

When you do not trust yourself,

you are not trusting Me.

To say that you trust My words

but do not trust your own,

is a lie.

You cannot feel faith

and cherish this lie.

I have made you as I meant you to be.

You must accept this

if you would go forward.

Even things you choose to
misunderstand as flaws,
you must accept them too.
There is only One Source,
and I Am eternal.
You are from that same source
and you are eternal.

The truth is not hidden.
It presents itself in countless ways.
But you will not hear until you listen.
This is the obstacle in your own path—
the habit of not-listening.
When you truly listen, truly attend
in the little moments of your life today,
much will be revealed to you.
When you truly listen to another person,
no matter who they are,
they will bless you.
When you have learned how to listen,
truly listen,
then you will receive the power
to truly speak.
It is for this purpose you have come.

There is always mystery. It is sacred.
Wade into the mystery as you would
wade into a meadow
deep with wildflowers.
Brush against all the kinds and ways
that beauty manifests itself
as mystery, wonder, and discovery.
Take back your sense of wonder.
Take back the joy of mystery,
magic, and secret gifts.
Know deeply and strongly that all these
wondrous gifts and marvelous surprises
are already yours by birthright.
Go out and find them.
Wade out into the ocean of
mystery and possibility
with the eager expectation

of a little child wading through
an infinite ocean of wildflowers,
and see what you find there.
It all belongs to you.

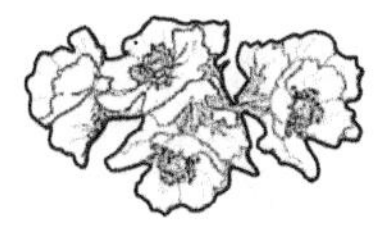

You have been told
there are only two choices in eternity—
love or fear.
You cannot have both;
you cannot go both ways.
You are still choosing fear
while asking for love.
That cannot work.
You must choose love, and only love.
It doesn't matter even
what things you do.
For as long as you choose fear,
you cannot accept love.
Love is waiting. Choose love.
Love will wait forever.
But should you choose love now,
it will come now.

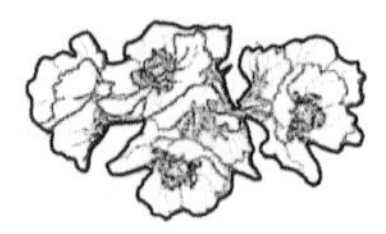

The only thing that is preventing you
from accepting love
and power and wisdom
is this chain of attachment to the past.
Let it go.
All that is past,
that was a part of your life,
gave its gift to you,
and you are the reason it came.
Now you are grown, it's time to let go
of anything and everything
you leaned upon in the past.
All people, all illusions,
all old hurts you've saved and left
unforgiven.
Forgive it all now.
Let all of it go,

and accept your own truth and power.
You can stall and make excuses forever,
or you can stand and say yes to God
now.

There is no fear in your heart,
it is only in your mind. Let it go.
You can let it go.
When you really want to be loved,
you can have that, in abundance.
All you have to do is give up all the
Reasons for not-loving.
Like pretty or not-pretty,
like old or young.
You don't need to be pretty
because you are beautiful.
You don't need to be young,
because you are eternal.
Make your heart a safe place for love to
come, and then welcome it without fear
when it does.

Beloved, your faith lies weak and faint.
I have promised you that
anything you ask believing,
you shall have it.
You ask, but you do not believe
this gift will be given.
I tell you this– the gift cannot come
until you believe.
Why do you not believe?
Know that this passage is temporary,
and when your heart is truly ready,
the universe will deliver the gift
almost immediately.
Open your heart a little each day.
And reach out gently, quietly,
from there.

Accept and love who you truly are.
This is the only thing you need,
to manifest the life of love and joy
that you have chosen.
Allow yourself to feel
your worthiness of love,
then all the boundless, endless love
that waits for you will come pouring in—
into your life, and then,
out into the world through you.
Take faith, and make
you heart's request to God,
clearly spoken.
Be willing to receive it,
and immediately, the gift is given.
Miracles are easy for God.
Accept, and they are easy for you too.

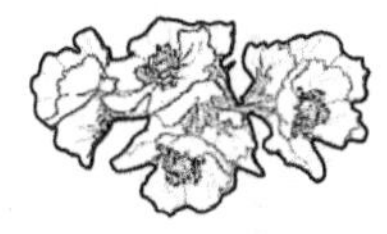

The ancient wisdom is learned
and re-learned
again and again.
Just as every child must struggle
first to stand, then to walk,
and then to run
with the swift sweep of wind in her face
and the ground beneath her feet
flying away
so effortlessly, so joyfully.
So too must every soul seek
and discover
who she truly is,
and when she does,
her joy is God's joy.

You have said that you feel invisible.
My child, nothing is visible in this world.
All of it is illusion
that we create in our minds,
and then God says "so be it"
and manifests it in this world.
But you are here as a translator,
and a teacher of God's love.
When you teach anything, teach love.

To be visible,
to be acknowledged in this world,
if that is what you want–
all you have to do is decide to be,
in your own mind, and you will be.
This is one of the easiest miracles.
Think of the good you could do

as a teacher
if you expressed your true self doing it.
Express your true feelings.
Express your true self, your Christ Self,
and I assure you,
you will not be invisible.

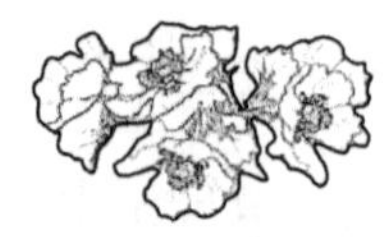

There are so many paths;
your heart is confused and troubled.
But I have not forsaken you.
Your heart will heal,
and your body will be
made whole and perfect,
just as you have asked.
I do not wish pain to any of my children.
You are my heart's joy.
I see you fall as you learn to walk.
I pick you up again.
And you begin again.
This is your learning-place.
Everywhere you will ever go
will be a learning-place.

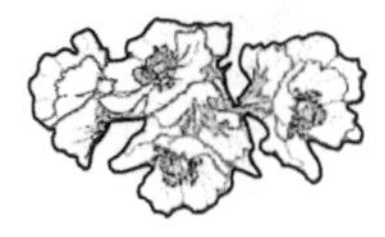

This passage is hard.
You are in a dark place
where you cannot see the light,
but the light is not gone
and not dimmed.
Pass through to the light
stronger than you were before.
Forgive yourself,
for that is the only real obstacle
in your life.
Take faith in yourself,
make constant and steadfast your faith,
no matter what comes.
It is this faith that empowers.

You know that death is not
the end of life,
it is only a turning point of the journey.
Those who leave us
don't grieve or cry,
so don't grieve or cry for them.
Be glad for they begin again.
You are not a human being that leaves
its body when it dies;
you are a celestial being that takes
residence in a human form
for a while.
It is God's pleasure to
adventure here as you.
You are not anything that dies.
Understand this,
and you will understand

that there is nothing here to fear.
Live your joy.
Do not question, but accept, and trust,
and allow all of life to bless you.

The darkness swallows the earth,
and it is night.
But morning will come again,
and the new day
will shine without fear
of the last night's shadows,
for they shall flee from
the light.

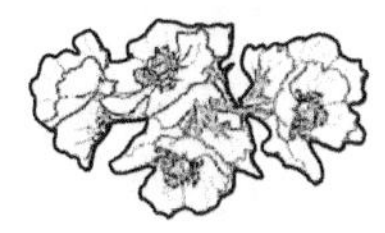

You are my child. I care for you.
You are wandering now.
You will come to a place
when the time is accomplished,
and it will be your rightful place.
These are the days of desolation,
but beyond the desert lies a garden,
wet with sweet rain.
It is beautiful there, where you shall be.
The path is trackless now,
like shifting sands
blown by winds of change.
But you are not lost,
even though it seems.
You are on course.
You are where you should be.

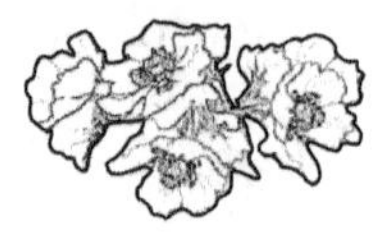

There are no guarantees
and no contracts
except My eternal sacred promise
to you and all of my children,
that I shall love you completely
and provide for you everything that
you need or want.
Ask and receive it as your birthright.
Know and believe that you are Mine
and I will never leave you.
I have never left you.
You are not now, never have been,
and never shall be
alone.

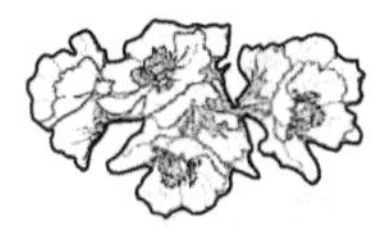

Beloved, You still have fear.
You must let that go.
When you enter fully into service,
you must make this choice
again and again,
to let go of fear,
and then it will let go of you.
You are Mine.
Whatever you do, I stand beside you.
You are firmly on your path now.
Simply know this, and faithfully follow
the feelings in your heart,
and you will be brought to your soul's
greatest treasure.
Lean not unto your own understanding.
You cannot understand all.
The learning is in the journey itself,

and is the purpose of having a path.
Take each step
confident in the knowledge
that I am Leading you.

Refuse to give power to the past.
Be done with your tears for anyone
whose path has crossed through yours.
Forgive all past sorrows
and let them go .
Nothing I send you has been sent to
hurt you,
but only to help you see that
you are not this.
You are not illness and death –
You are life and health and abundance.
Know this, and remember it.
When fear catches at your sleeve,
pull away, and say to the fear
"Be gone from me~
I Am a daughter of God."

The love is there. The power is there.
These things are already in you.
Truly, every gift you can imagine
is already given to you.
All That Is, is Mine to give you,
and I will withhold nothing from you.
Only ask and believe.
Nothing more is needed than faith.
Trust Me to give you
the greatest of love,
the greatest of care,
and the beautiful health you have
asked for.
I am healing you now.
Have faith.

Do you doubt that I shall heal
my daughter whom I have loved
and protected since your birth?
I cannot heal your doubt.
I cannot give this gift unless
you are willing to accept it.
Therefore do not worry and plead.
Practice your Faith,
and trust Me to provide
all the best possible blessings,
forthis is My desire for you.
Know this and remember it,
hold it in your heart.
Whenever fear tries to come,
speak your faith aloud
and say "My Father God is healing me—
I am whole and perfect and beautiful"

and everything that you wish
to be healed, will be healed.
Your challenge now is to heal yourself
through Me.
Then you will heal others,
because I will heal them through you.

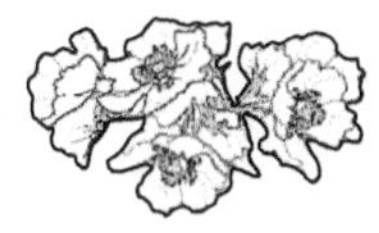

Beloved, do not be afraid
to walk through this door,
to leave behind whatever is past.
When you let go,
you are not losing anything,
you are not giving anything up.
You are releasing old things
you don't need any more,
to make room for the new things
that you want and deserve.
You think the old way
must have great value,
because it did once. No. Let it go.
That was then, and this is now.
This is the holy moment.

You weep because you are walking away
from something you loved,
that ended.
There is a Nothing now,
where a Something used to be.
What you loved has not died,
but has changed where it lives,
it grows and changes,
and so do you.
The love you gave is not lost or wasted.
It goes on forever,
like ripples on the water,
it spreads out and touches
many more than you know.

As you leave, go gracefully.
All can be forgiven now,
set free and clear.
Take no anger with you as you go.
Carry no baggage of regret,
for you have done well.
It does not matter who knows or not,
because God knows.
Even a prison is beautiful
when you walk away.
As you leave any part of your life
that is ending,
even when it ends with pain,
rejoice in gratitude,
for your lessons are now well-learned,
and your apprenticeship is done.

What you are feeling is grieving for
the death of your false self.
You were loyal to it because
for the while you were in it, it was you.
Now it is not you any longer.
This may seem like a loss, but It is not.
Your Self is eternal,
but it needs to grow,
to become always more
than it was before.
What you are now is
all that you ever were,
and all that you are becoming.
Trust in this truth.
Your old self was true once,
but you have outgrown it
and it must be shed

like the sheaf of last year's skin
that the dear little grass snakes
cast off each spring
because it is too small for them
now that they have grown.

Let this go. Your path goes on
and nothing is lost.
You were sent into this circle of lives
to bless them and to help them grow.
You have done that.
In doing so,
you have learned about yourself.
Their gift to you is real,
but it came from within you,
not from them.
It has always been
within you.

Your life is rich.
You have wealth of love,
wealth of spirit,
Every good thing
that gives your heart joy,
what ever you want,
God wants that for you.
Every good desire comes from God.
God shares your joy,
just as He shares your sorrow.
You are a manifestation
of the heart and mind of God,
and so you are worthy.
It is the Father's pleasure to give
good gifts to His children.
Each one is His favorite.

First, know that You are Mine.
Never doubt My
complete and eternal love for you.
Know that you are in My care
every moment
throughout eternity,
and know that you are safe.
Nothing can touch you, for you are
Mine.
Your path is one we chose together,
and we choose together each day.
There are many choices,
and infinite opportunities for joy.
It is My will that you shall have joy,
because you have chosen it.
It is My will that you shall have health,
because you have chosen it.

It is My will that you shall have beauty,
because you have chosen it.
It is My will that you shall have love,
because you have chosen it.
You have only to ask and believe.

This is what you must learn again:
to ask for help and offer help,
to ask for love and offer love.
Be ready and know that sometimes
your love will fall on fallow ground.
But some of the times
it will take root and grow.
It is important that you share your gifts,
even if the world
does not seem to want them.
It does need them.
Sleep now; it is enough.
Know that the spring will come.
Look forward in faith and know
that you are loved.

Each soul has chosen, and each soul
has received as it has asked.
Honor the choices of your
brothers and sisters
and simply love them through
whatever events
their souls have chosen.
I give my children joy because
it pleasures me to do so.
To see my children joyful
is my greatest joy.
Therefore do not waste my gifts of joy
by thinking I would give you a gift
that I do not want you to have.
And do not refuse the gifts of joy
just because you have seen
others do so.

I tell you again– Your life is yours.
It is my gift to you.
Choose life, and live it fully and
as joyfully as you will.
Choose love, and spread it generously
wherever you will,
in whatever ways you will.

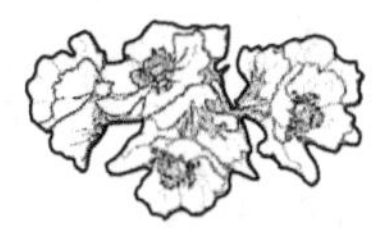

On the other side,
where the unseen shines
in beauty so intense it would blind
mortal eyes,
all questions are answered and
all truths are known.
But you are here, on this side now,
and have chosen to be.
You ask me to tell you what to do,
as if there were only one right thing.
I tell you again,
there are no wrong answers.
You learned to paint with dark colors
because that was the paintbox
your parents showed to you.
But there is an infinity of colors
you can have. Take them.

Love the life that you have,
and more life will come.
You can change it, or not, but first
see it as the gift and blessing
that it is.

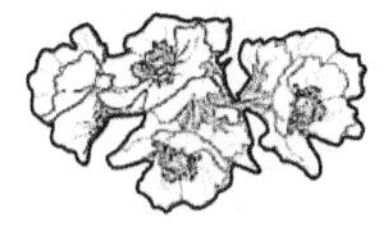

Today is a gift to you, a clean slate
on which you will write the future.
You can be today
that which you desire to become,
for it is ready to be manifest.
My love will never fail you,
and your Faith will make you whole,
and no evil or harm can ever befall you
so long as you
put your whole faith and trust in Me.
I Am the Father who created you.
My wish and will is that
you shall have joy and love and
abundance.
You stand now at the door.

Open it.

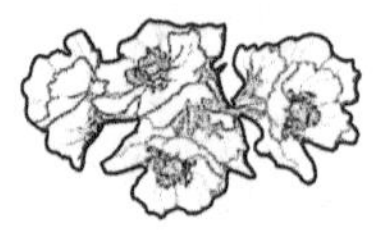

I am with you always,
even as the living air.
Look up at the sky.
No matter where you go or
where you are,
it is always there.
Even if you forget, it is there yet.
In the day it's filled with sailing clouds
of unspeakable beauty.
In the night it's filled with
billions of calm stars,
gleaming so cool and distant,
and yet, they are suns, each one,
they are fire.
God keeps a place for every star,
and God keeps a place for you.
Take your place, Beloved.

God will hold your place for you.
No matter what appears or seems to be,
this is the truth:
Your place in God's heart is secure.
Your place in God's plan is certain.
And your place in this world
is safe for you to be.
It is the place your soul has chosen,
and your soul has not made a mistake.

About the Author

V. Blakeman Vaughn is an essayist and
practical mystic with spiritual roots
in traditional Christian Protestant Faith,
living gratefully in the Pacific Northwest
of the United States.

About Darkhorse Press
New Thought Library

New Thought Library continues the time-
honored tradition of American authors
and self-publishers, thinkers, and writers
like Ralph Waldo Emerson,
Henry David Thoreau, Walt Whitman, and
others of the American Transcendentalist
movement, as well as our contemporaries in
New Thought. Independent Small Press
Publishers have always been a respected part
of American Literature.

www.ingramcontent.com/pod-product-compliance
Lightning Source LLC
Chambersburg PA
CBHW071504030726
47593CB00003B/1139